# THE
# HIGHLAND RAILWAY
# IN RETROSPECT

The Highland Railway station pilot at Perth, shunting an H.R. carriage at the north end of the station. 4-4-0T No. 58B has a Jones louvred chimney with a flared top.                    *J.T. Rutherford*

*Front Cover*
A Highland Railway train leaving Perth, passing the ticket platform, and on the right, the H.R. locomotive shed. The engine is No. 132 *Loch Naver*.
                                        *D.L.G.H. collection*

# THE
# HIGHLAND RAILWAY
# IN RETROSPECT

By
**D.L.G. Hunter, C.Eng.**

**MOORFOOT PUBLISHING**
**EDINBURGH**

ISBN 0 906606 14 4

Cover design by Tony Steers.

Published in 1988 by
 Moorfoot Publishing,
 PO Box 506,
 South West Postal District,
 Edinburgh 10.


Printed by

 Kelso Graphics,
 The Knowes,
 Kelso.

# CONTENTS

# INTRODUCTION

The history of the Highland Railway Company has been well documented, as also have its locomotives, carriages and wagons, but there are many other features of the Highland Railway, its equipment and operations, which made it so intriguing to many, even to some who never saw it until after it was part of the LMS, or even BR.

The Highland cannot be regarded as anything other than a trunk line, yet most of it was single track. In spite of penetrating so much mountainous terrain it had only three short tunnels, although it could boast a good complement of large bridges and viaducts, and a swing-bridge. There were other unusual features: where else on a main-line was a private passenger locomotive in frequent use?

This book is an attempt to highlight some of the unusual features of the Highland Railway and its operations, and to offer illustrations of some of its structures and equipment, which may be of use to a model-maker. The scene is set with a brief description of the main-lines, but it is not a "history" although a sketch of the company's origin is shown on page 73: nor is it a catalogue of the rolling-stock. Some small parts of it appeared in *The Highland Railway Company and its Constituents and Successors 1855-1955,* published by the Stephenson Locomotive Society, which can be recommended as one of the most useful books on that railway. Space must preclude mention of all the variations in the working arrangements quoted. So far as possible, use of illustrations which have appeared elsewhere, has been avoided, but in a few cases no suitable alternative could be found, and it is hoped that inclusion of this small number of perhaps familiar views can be excused. Illustrations of locomotives and rolling-stock are prolific in other works so that only a very small leavening of such views appears herein.

For much help with illustrations thanks are due to my friends Graham Langmuir, James Stevenson, and the late George Ellis. Many interesting matters have been brought to my attention by David Stirling, whose help in many ways is much appreciated. The Special Notice to the Staff of December 29th 1922 was kindly loaned by N.A.H. Tindall.

# THE MAIN LINE FROM THE SOUTH

A first encounter with the Highland would often take place at the large and busy General Station at Perth, jointly owned by the Caledonian, North British, and Highland companies. Here the Highland's olive-green engines and carriages, most of the latter with vertical matchboard sides and ends, would be quite a change for someone from the south, as too, would be the third-class carriage upholstery of brown with a pattern picked out in black and often described as "autumn tints". The Highland's station pilot at Perth, in later years the Jones 4-4-0T No 58B, would fascinate with its outside Allan framing and cylinders, low boiler and louvred chimney, the last-named being a smoke-lifting arrangement which one would see on many older engines on the Highland.

The Highland passenger engines carried names rivalling those on the North British engines, and in contrast to the almost complete lack of names on their Caledonian counterparts. One would likely soon see such names as *Ben-y-Gloe, Ben Alligan, Cluny Castle, Dunvegan Castle, Urquhart Castle, Brodie Castle, Darnaway Castle, Foulis Castle, Beaufort Castle, Duncraig Castle, Loch Moy, Loch an dorb, Loch Garry, Loch Fannich, Clan Campbell, Clan Fraser,* or *Clan Munro,* all of which were based at Perth in 1918-19, where the Highland Railway had their own locomotive shed on the down side of the line just north of the station. It had eight roads or stalls. *Glen Truim* and *Glen Bruar* were older engines then at Blair Atholl. This, however, is not the place to list all the Highland names and numbers, which are fully documented in several other works.

After running on the Caledonian main-line for 7¼ miles, the Highland diverged on to its own line at Stanley, where the junction layout was unusual though logical. The down platform was an island, the up side of the Highland loop using its outer face and giving in effect right-hand running. The inner face continued northwards along the Highland line beyond the junction so allowing a down Highland train to stand clear of the Caledonian main-line should it have to await an up train coming off the single-line. There was a speed limit here of 15 mph for Highland trains. (See diagram on p75).

The journey northwards continued on the single-line with its crossing loops at most stations and some elsewhere, where one might have to wait for a train approaching from the opposite direction. Seen from the station platform, the engine driver would give up the tablet for the section of single-line which he had just left and in due course receive another one for the section ahead without which he must not proceed, and the same would be seen to be done in regard to the train going in the opposite direction. If the train was not stopping at the station the exchange of tablets would be effected by the exchanging apparatus on the engine and at the lineside. All of this would also provide fresh interest for one used to double-track main-lines. True, there were some sections of double-track on the Highland, which we will come to in due course.

The first tunnel, Kingswood - although sometimes in earlier days called Murthly tunnel- was reached soon after the first Highland station at Murthly, and the second tunnel, known as Inver, lay a short distance beyond the next station, Dunkeld. Then, after Dalguise station, the River Tay was crossed by a large lattice girder bridge with castellated piers. Just beyond it was Guay platform where there was no crossing loop and this would bring us to Ballinluig junction where the Aberfeldy branch diverged westwards. The latter commenced as a double-line junction from the south end of the Ballinluig crossing-loop, with the platform in the vee, the branch becoming single-line beyond its platform, before crossing the River Tummel and then the Tay again by similar bridges. (See diagram on p76). There was no platform on the down side of the branch but there was a crossover so situated that the branch engine could run round its train at the platform without fouling the main-line. A through carriage between Perth and Aberfeldy was provided on some trains, and the shunting of this was inevitably somewhat complicated.

The next station, Pitlochry, was quite an important one, after which the railway ran through the Pass of Killiecrankie by viaduct and tunnel, the latter being the third and last tunnel on the line, before reaching Killiecrankie station. In order that trains would not be brought to a stand in the tunnel, the Killiecrankie home-signal was located at the south entrance to the tunnel: shunting movements were allowed to pass it at danger.

Next we come to Blair Atholl. Outside the small shed behind the north end of the down platform, one or two engines would be seen waiting for piloting or banking duties up "the hill", probably one or more of the fine 0-6-4Ts among them. At the end of the down platform here there were two water columns so spaced that the two locomotives of a double-headed train could both take water at the same time. We have now reached the first section of double-line, a 23¼ mile stretch mostly at 1 in 70 up to the 1,484 ft summit at Drumochter, the highest point on a main-line in the country.

Just before Struan station, 4½ miles from Blair Atholl, there was a bridge carrying the line over the river Garry and through the arch of which a roadway passed under the line and also crossed the river. When this section of the original single-line was doubled between 1900 and 1909, a separate lattice girder bridge was provided for the second line, spoiling an otherwise picturesque setting. Two miles before the summit Dalnaspidal station was reached.

Trains not already double-headed would often take a pilot engine from Blair Atholl, and this might come off at Dalnaspidal if the train was booked to stop there, or it would continue over the summit and down to Dalwhinnie. Although the Board of Trade did not favour the use of banking engines pushing at the rear of a train, the practice pertained at Blair Atholl from where the banking engine would push to Dalnaspidal. In 1908 it was laid down that the banking engine must be coupled to the train which had to stop at Dalnaspidal for it to be detached and a goods train's couplings checked. If further assistance was required the assisting engine had to be transferred to the front of the train as a pilot before proceeding beyond Dalnaspidal and over the summit. This was not always necessary, since for the final two miles from Dalnaspidal to the summit, trains got a good start on an easy length through and beyond the station.

From Dalwhinnie it was single-line and crossing loops again down the Spey valley to Newtonmore, Kingussie, Kincraig, and Aviemore. Up trains would take a pilot engine if required from Kingussie which would be detached at Dalnaspidal or at Blair Atholl as convenient, although after the First World War up trains were piloted through from Aviemore instead of from Kingussie.

When the direct line from Aviemore to Inverness was opened in 1898, Aviemore

8

Two engines watering at Blair Atholl. The provision of two water columns, one for each engine of a double-headed train, saved much time. The pilot is No. 132 *Loch Naver* and the other engine an unidentified member of the Castle class.*D.L.G.H. collection*

One of the Highland Railway's series of postcard views. This one is of Drumochter summit, 1484 above sea level and alternatively known in earlier days as the Sow of Atholl.                    *D.L.G.H. collection*

Dalguise viaduct. The lattice girder bridge with castellated piers over the River Tay between Dalguise and Guay.

*J.L. Stevenson collection*

Pitlochry station. Typical of the earlier stone-built two-block and verandah station buildings with corbie-stepped gables.

*G.E. Langmuir collection*

The bridges at Struan. The lower bridge over the River Garry carries a minor road and the upper one the original single main-line. The steel bridge carrying the second track added later is behind it, and rather spoiled an otherwise pleasant scene.

*J.L. Stevenson collection*

The long lattice girder viaduct over the River Findhorn at Tomatin, built by Fairbairn & Sons. *J.L. Stevenson*

became an important junction station, the up platform then becoming an island, and a bay provided at the north end of the down platform. As at Blair Atholl, there were two water columns at the end of the platform. Taking the direct line, there was a steep climb from Carrbridge, 5¼ miles at 1 in 60-70 to a summit at Slochd where there was a crossing loop but no station, then down equally steep grades for 12¼ miles to Millburn junction at Inverness. The last 10½ miles from Daviot to Millburn junction were built as a double-line.

This was an approach best seen early on a summer morning when the rising sun bathed a delightful scene over the Beauly Firth, now alas much altered. A train running down this last stretch at night, with sparks flying from all its brake blocks was, in recent times, thought by the crew of an aircraft to be on fire. On this length there was, among others, a long lattice girder viaduct at Tomatin and a large masonry one at Culloden, while at Moy station there was a private waiting-room for The Mackintosh of Moyhall. Many trains were piloted from Aviemore up to Slochd where a stop would be made to detach the pilot, and so also were trains piloted from Inverness up to Slochd. Two dozen spraggs — sticks used to jam wheels on runaway vehicles — were kept spaced beside the line on each side of Slochd summit in case of emergencies. Until 1907, all goods trains between Perth and Inverness included a brake van in the middle of the train as well as one at the end.

Tomatin station. One of the later style of buildings of timber construction with hipped gables. The well-known Tomatin distillery was nearby and was the source of much of the station's traffic. *D.L.G.H. collection*

The Carrbridge accident of June 18th 1914, when the bridge over the Baddengorm burn collapsed. H.R. carriage in the foreground and a Caledonian one beyond. *D.L.G.H. collection*

Despite all its difficulties with so much single-line, the Highland escaped spectacular accident apart from that near Carrbridge on June 18th 1914 following a sudden flood which undermined a bridge over the Baddengorm burn, causing it to collapse under a train. Five people were killed and nine injured. Traffic had to be diverted to the old route by Dava but the bridge was quickly reconstructed and the line reopened for passenger trains on July 13th. Until the works consolidated, up trains were stopped by hand signal at a point to the north and thereafter proceeded at walking pace over the bridge. Down trains were similarly cautioned to walking pace but on account of the gradient were not brought to a stand. Goods trains did not return to the new route until later.

The Highland did have its mishaps of course. The first to be recorded was the inadvertant diversion of the train from Nairn into the locomotive depot instead of the passenger station at Inverness in May 1856, although a similar diversion on to the Harbour branch is said to have occurred before this.

Some accidents arose from the methods of working. Further north particularly, in such sparse country, trains were few, some of them being run "mixed", i.e. passenger and goods vehicles together. The Board of Trade disliked mixed trains and stipulated that, if they were run, the passenger carriages should always be marshalled next to the engine so that they were connected to the automatic brake system. For shunting wagons at the stations en route it naturally suited the company better to put the wagons at the front - and this they continued to do - for Inverness was a long way from London! Mixed trains on the Aberfeldy, Fochabers, Hopeman, Fort George, Dornoch, and Lybster branches were supposed to be limited to ten wagons.

An interesting example of some of the remarkable things sometimes done in earlier days occurred on November 9th 1871 when a passenger train from Forres was struggling up to Dava in a snowstorm. The pilot engine was to come off at Dava, but the driver of the train engine reckoned he would need assistance for the 2½ miles to the summit beyond. He sent his fireman forward to so advise the driver of the pilot engine, and shortly before reaching Dava, and while still on the move, to uncouple the pilot engine which then speeded forward into the "wrong" side of the loop there. Clearly the pointsman had known what he was expected to do when he saw the pilot engine approaching detached, so that releasing a pilot engine in this way without stopping the train cannot have been unusual. In this instance however, when the train, not booked to stop at Dava, passed through, the pilot engine set off out of the loop it was on. Accelerating, the pilot followed after the train much faster than the 10mph at which the latter was travelling, and on catching it up - to act as an unofficial banker - more than half a mile farther on, struck it rather hard. No material damage was done and the incident only came to light because a few passengers and the guard complained of injury when the train stopped at the next station, Grantown. This was not the only occasion when the practice came to light.

In the land of the "mountain dew" it is perhaps not surprising that an occasional lapse from grace should occur even among train crews, but so far as can be ascertained, no serious accident resulted therefrom on the Highland. The story is told of a certain stationmaster's kindly advice to a slightly errant trainman "You'll go to perdition if you keep on the way you're going", whereupon the reply was "That's all right Mr ---, is the signal off?"

Highland signalling was interesting, and the signals themselves were different

Elevated signal wires at Altnabreac. The run to the signal cabin across the tracks is also completely protected to obviate difficulties in a snowstorm. *D.L.G.H.*

from those on other Scottish railways, the posts being of timber instead of lattice iron and with a long spiked finial, though in later years a few lattice iron posts appeared here and there. Most of the equipment was supplied by McKenzie & Holland Ltd., but some came from Dutton & Co. The lamps were mounted on a vertical slide and wound up and down by a small windlass at the bottom of the post although ladders were also provided. Skeleton arms with a letter S fixed to them were used for shunting movements, their lamp being fitted with a stencil plate showing S. About 1898 "fish-tail" stencils were tried in the lamps of distant signals, and in 1903 the last of the white lights hitherto used for the "off" indication of signals were being changed to green.

Signal cabins were usually of timber construction with ridge roofs of corrugated iron although slates were sometimes used; a stove was provided for heating. Ground disc signals for siding movements were of the revolving type and sometimes operated from the blades of trap points at the exit from a siding. In the earlier days, this was the usual practice. At a few places, this type of signal was mounted on top of a post, up to ten feet or so high. Another feature at exposed places was the carrying of signal wires on timber posts up to 15ft high to keep them clear of drifting snow. For the same reason point rodding, cranks, compensators, and detectors were at many places enclosed in timber troughing. At a number of non-block stations two-way semaphore signals, operated by a hand lever on the post, were provided to indicate to drivers when a conditional stop was required to pick up passengers. Examples were located at Glencarron Platform on the Skye line, Invershin, and the private platforms in Sutherland at Salzcraggie and Borrobol. Broomhill was also provided with these signals, as was Guay on the main-line to Perth. This last-named could be used by the stationmaster to stop the mid-day down Inverness train if he had passengers for north of Blair Atholl; the local trains between Perth and Blair Atholl were booked to stop at Guay. At Glencarron Platform, if only a mail bag had to be put on or off, the train was not to stop but merely to slow down for this to be done. We will return to the operation of signalling later.

Inverness station from the east in 1908, showing platforms 1,2,3, and 4, with a Perth express about to leave No. 2. The building on the right is the Lochgorm locomotive works with the Station signal cabin beyond. Note the carriage truck in the loading dock at the end of platforms 1 and 2. *D.L.G.H. collection*

## INVERNESS AND KEITH

Another unusual feature was that peculiar station at Inverness; or was it really two stations? It was like a triangle upside-down with the two legs at the bottom not effectively connected. The right-hand leg, the original part, came in from Welsh's Bridge signal cabin, and the left-hand leg from Rose Street signal cabin. Linking these two directly were the "Ross-shire lines" without any platforms, the middle of the triangle being occupied by the locomotive works known as Lochgorm. Around Welsh's Bridge - the bridge itself having disappeared in 1895 - and between it and Millburn junction were ample sidings, with the Needlefield carriage works on the north side. The distinctive locomotive depot, built in 1864, was on the south side. Three tracks led to a turntable around which the shed building was arranged as a three-quarters segment of a roundhouse. The middle approach track ran under a large masonry archway incorporating a hidden water tank.

From Millburn junction the original main-line led off eastwards over a fairly level course to Nairn and Forres where it turned south to climb steeply over Dava summit and down to Aviemore. The Great North of Scotland Railway's Speyside branch came in at a point between Broomhill and Boat of Garten to run alongside the Highland line for some three miles to the latter station, the two single lines giving the impression of a double line. Broomhill station, which had no crossing loop, had

17

a level-crossing through its platform near the north end with a moveable piece to fill the gap, but wherever possible, trains were to stop towards the south end and clear of this gap. Forres would provide a pilot engine, if required, which would normally be detached at Dava but on occasion would continue on to Grantown and assist a train from there back over Dava summit to Forres. The climb from Forres up to Dava was however another hill up which banking engines were used for assistance. If a goods train was not so banked, it was to be worked "double-block" so that in case of breakaway the signalman at the intermediate station of Dunphail had a chance of interception by diverting it into a siding, or if seen to be "running hard", to derail it.

The Inverness & Nairn Railway was the earliest part of the Highland Railway, opened for passenger traffic on November 5th 1855. Goods traffic commenced later, on December 1st. Soon the Inverness & Aberdeen Junction Railway continued the line eastwards from Nairn to Forres and Elgin, and then with some appreciable gradients and a large plate girder bridge (later replaced by a lattice girder one) at the bottom of a dip over the River Spey at Orton, to Keith, from where the Great North of Scotland Railway continued to Aberdeen. The original plate girder bridge

The train destination indicator on platform 7 at Inverness lasted many years into L.M.S. days. The arm displayed reads Muir of Ord, Fortrose, Kyle of Lochalsh.                                                                    *D.L.G.H.*

was the subject of much argument between the H.R. and the Board of Trade and led to much delay in the opening of this part of the line. Trains were apparently worked over it before the Board of Trade finally gave its blessing.

Forres was a triangular station with a level-crossing leading to it over the leg between Forres South and Forres East, and on which there was a short platform which saw little use. The Highland station at Elgin was a typical one with passing loop but at the East cabin a line diverged to the left to serve the one through main-line platform of the Great North of Scotland's more important-looking station. It was connected to the Highland station by a footpath. These routes were all single lines although the first 6¼ miles from Millburn junction to Dalcross had been doubled as early as 1864.

Back to Inverness, and westwards from Rose Street signal cabin it was only ¼ mile to Ness Viaduct signal cabin where single line commenced on the route to the north and west. The Harbour branch descended from, and alongside, the "Ross-shire lines", leading through a gate at the bottom across the roadway on to the quay. Locomotives were not allowed to pass the gate, wagons having to be moved on the quay by horses, which in earlier days often worked the whole of the branch.

At one time, trains from the south and east, and from the north, ran into their respective sides of Inverness station, but if there were any through vehicles on them they first stopped outside to detach these vehicles which were then worked over the Ross-shire lines and backed on to the front of the train waiting at the other side of the station. There is a story of an interested railway officer from the south who, venturing to remark that "At Euston we would have -" was cut short with "Euston! Euston! What's Euston mon, it's naethin' tae this station". Later it became the practice for trains making forward connections to be taken over the Ross-shire lines and then backed into the opposite side so as to be alongside the connecting train on the other side of the platform, which was really a very sensible arrangement.

As already mentioned, the two arms of the Inverness station were not really connected. However, it was in fact possible to transfer a vehicle between the two sides of the station by means of a siding from the east side alongside the wall of the locomotive workshops which connected with the nearest platform road, No. 5, on the west side not far from its buffer stop. The connection was controlled from the small "Locomotive Cabin" alongside the Lochgorm works and the small Station Cabin in the vee. This was only done in special circumstances, e.g. for the through mail van on May 21-23 1898 when the Ross-shire lines were under engineers' possession. Considerable track and signalling alterations were being carried out at Inverness station and approaches during 1898 in connection with the completion of the new direct line from Aviemore.

Very few trains ever passed Inverness without stopping, although from 1911 to 1915 on Tuesdays only in July, August, and September, there was a train which did so. This started from Aviemore, connecting with the morning train from Perth and the south, and ran to Strathpeffer, stopping only at Dingwall. In June it ran on Tuesdays as a through train from Edinburgh and Glasgow with stops only at Perth, Kingussie, Aviemore and Dingwall. There was no similar train in the opposite direction.

Clachnaharry swing-bridge, partly opened. A view looking towards Inverness taken in modern times. The signal cabin is a few yards behind the camera. The Black Isle can be seen in the background across the Beauly Firth. *D.L.G.H.*

# TO THE NORTH AND WEST

From the Ness Viaduct signal cabin the single-line ran westwards over easy grades towards Beauly and Dingwall with fine views across the Beauly Firth to the Black Isle (so called, although it is not an island). The first point of interest however was the swing-bridge over the Caledonian Canal at Clachnaharry, in those days operated by hand gear.

Immediately beyond was Clachnaharry station, still on single-line, but in 1913-14 the line beyond Clachnaharry was doubled as far as Clunes. Previously there had been a crossing loop at Bruichnain just beyond Clachnaharry and 2¼ miles from Ness Viaduct signal cabin. The double line commenced beyond the bridge under the main road some distance beyond the platform but the points were located near the platform within the working distance of the signal cabin, with interlaced track to beyond the road bridge. A bell-push was provided at the up home signal so that a driver could indicate his presence there to the signalman. Just after the Highland became part of the LMS, this arrangement was altered, and the points moved to beyond the road bridge.

The Clachnaharry stationmaster was in charge of the swing-bridge, but this station was closed in 1913 and thereafter the signalman was in control of the swing-bridge, over which there was a speed limit of 8mph.

A short branch to the canal basin at Muirtown left the main-line between Ness Viaduct and Clachnaharry with access gained by inserting the tablet for the section in the ground frame at the junction, this action also releasing the lock on the swing-bridge so that it could be opened for shipping while the train was on the branch. The tablet could not be regained from the ground frame unless the bridge was in its normal closed position. A daily goods train from and to Inverness ran at a quiet time of day.

Reaching Beauly, the line turned northwards to Muir of Ord, where the Black Isle branch went off eastwards to Fortrose. Most of the Highland's branches were quite short, only this one, the Aberfeldy branch and the Lybster Light Railway, were of any great length, 13½, 8¾, and 13¾ miles respectively, although there had been another 13¾ miles long from Keith to Portessie. The last-mentioned was closed, due to lack of staff, on August 9th 1915, and the rails etc. later used elsewhere.

At Dingwall the Skye line went off westwards. Dingwall station was something like that at Aviemore, with the up platform an island and a bay on the down side for the Strathpeffer branch train. What would have become another branch, the Cromarty & Dingwall Light Railway, was also to have commenced at Dingwall, but instead, Conon, the next station to the south, was decided upon for the junction. Construction along the north side of the Black Isle commenced from Cromarty in 1902 but proceeded very slowly, being abandoned on the outbreak of war in 1914, when the two miles of track laid by then were lifted for use elsewhere.

The North line to Wick and Thurso continued on easy grades through arable country to reach the Kyle of Sutherland, crossed by a high lattice girder bridge near the confluence of the Rivers Oykell and Shin. Now inland and in Sutherland, the

21

line climbed at 1 in 72 to Lairg, the railhead station for the mail buses to the northwest of the country. There was some fine scenery at and beyond Invershin, the line being carried high above the gorge of the Shin, with a splendid view up Strath Oykell to the mountain peaks in the west. Beyond Lairg the countryside is moorland again, and after another 2¾ miles at 1 in 70, Acheilidh summit is reached, followed by seven miles down at 1 in 80 to Rogart station, with a crossing-loop half-way down.

The viaduct over the Kyle of Sutherland at Invershin. This fine view was taken after the passing of the Highland Railway Company but the railway scene remains unaltered. Invershin station adjoins the viaduct to the right, the station buildings being typical of the early ones in the north. They are now derelict. The large building in the centre background is Carbisdale Castle, one-time home of the Duchess of Sutherland and later used as a youth hostel. *J.L. Stevenson collection*

Culrain station, which is just out of view to the left of the previous illustration, half a mile from Invershin station. The station accommodation is a small building of timber construction.

*G.E. Langmuir collection*

The coast was regained at The Mound. This station had one platform on the up side and was not a crossing point for passenger trains, the loop being usable only by goods trains. The Dornoch branch diverged here, crossing the embankment or Mound over Loch Fleet, and using a platform at a slightly lower level at the back of the main-line platform. The Dornoch branch was a Light Railway: where it crossed public highways the gates were protected by a single pointed signal arm which served for both directions.

On the main-line it was then easy going along the coast to Golspie, Brora, and Helmsdale. It may be mentioned that the length between Golspie and Helmsdale was originally the Duke of Sutherland's Railway, built at his own expense. Where it passed in front of Dunrobin Castle, a cut and cover tunnel had been intended but no tunnel was made. From Helmsdale another big detour inland was taken, climbing through pleasant country, but becoming ever more desolate, to a summit at the County March where the line, now heading towards the coast again, entered Caithness.

One of the Dornoch Light Railway level-crossing signals, where the track crossed the road at the other end of the Loch Fleet embankment. The stripe was originally a chevron matching the point of the arm.                    *D.L.G.H.*

The Mound junction station, with the Dornoch branch curving off to the right over the Loch Fleet embankment. Passenger trains could not be crossed here, the loop being available only to goods trains.
*D.L.G.H. collection*

At Georgemass junction, locally "The Georgemass", the branch from Thurso trailed in, and then it was an easy run through rough pastures to the terminus at Wick. The Lybster branch, another Light Railway, joined in just outside the station. Up trains sometimes took a pilot engine from Georgemass to Forsinard or Helmsdale as might be convenient for its return. Similarly, pilot engines were available at Helmsdale if required to assist northwards to Altnabreac or southwards to Lairg. It would sometimes be arranged for the pilot, after being turned at Lairg, to proceed to Bonar Bridge if a goods train required assistance from there.

A yard lamp, lit by gas, at Thurso. The passenger platform can be seen in the background with overall roof at the buffer-stop end. The goods shed is on the right.                                                                    *D.L.G.H.*

"The Georgemass". The Thurso branch train is on the left and the Wick-Inverness train on the right. The somewhat unusual layout is shown on page    .*D.L.G.H. collection*

At Fodderty junction, 2½ miles on the Skye line from Dingwall, the Strathpeffer branch diverged. The Skye line then encountered a tremendous climb, mostly at 1 in 50, over the Raven Rock summit. So steep was this length that, for fear of possible runaway, no train was allowed to come down from Achterneed station (which originally served Strathpeffer), half way up the hill, unless the line between Dingwall and Strathpeffer was entirely clear. After a level stretch before Garve, plenty of climbing followed to Luib summit and then down to Strathcarron, from where it was fairly level, although tortuous, to the terminus at the Kyle of Lochalsh. This last length still provides some spectacular scenery.

Duncraig platform, situated on this stretch, was quite short and on the outside of a sharp curve, so the guard had to wave his green flag to the driver from a window on the other side of the train, i.e. on the inside of the curve. Trains stopped here only on personal application by the tenant of the adjoining castle to the stationmaster at either Plockton or Strome Ferry, or to the guard of a train.

As originally built, the terminus of the Skye line was at Strome Ferry, and for ten years the Highland Railway had run a steamer service from Strome Ferry to Portree and Stornoway before relinquishing such activities in favour of David MacBrayne. It was then another seventeen years before the railway was extended to Kyle of Lochalsh which, in 1897, became the embarkation point. The ferry across Loch Carron at Strome remained, there being no road along the south side of the loch between Strathcarron and Strome Ferry until quite recent times. In earlier days of motoring, conveyance of motor cars by train between Strathcarron and Strome Ferry was often preferred to using the ferry, and some carriage trucks were kept ready at these stations for that traffic.

The Kyle of Lochalsh terminus, with the Isle of Skye in the background.
*D.L.G.H. collection*

The company's brief ownership of steamers had ended strangely. Of their last two ships, the S.S. *Ferret* was, pending sale, chartered for six months to a "firm" that proved bogus. The ship was stolen, its name changed, and it was eventually traced in Australia where possession was regained and a good sale effected.

Strathpeffer station: a larger building with saw-tooth glass verandah over the platform. The station is now a craft centre with a garden laid out on the trackbed.

*J.L. Stevenson collection*

Strathpeffer was, as already observed, at the end of a short branch from Fodderty junction on the Skye line. The Highland Railway built a fine hotel at Strathpeffer Spa in 1911 and provided a small Albion charabanc to take passengers the short distance to it from the station and to take them on excursions. During the summer months the stationmaster at Kyle of Lochalsh sent a weather report to Strathpeffer station every morning, and this was duly displayed in the hotel, although this public advice had to be suspended during the First World War.

The Highland Railway owned another three hotels at Inverness, Dornoch, and Kyle of Lochalsh, and was part owner of the Station Hotel at Perth - and very good hotels they were too. There were also refreshment rooms at the stations at Kingussie, Keith, Forres, Inverness, Dingwall, Bonar Bridge, and Kyle of Lochalsh. At Achnasheen, about mid-way between Dingwall and Kyle of Lochalsh, and where most trains crossed, there was a small privately run "hotel" in part of the station building. It was quite a ritual at this station. Trains were allowed a three minute stop here but it is unlikely that this was ever sufficient time to herd the thirsty passengers back into their trains!

The Highland believed in the value of publicity and issued a comprehensive and very informative Tourist Guide. They opened a public office in Edinburgh and also one in Glasgow. Travellers were asked to ensure that their tickets were routed "via Dunkeld". The only named train, however, was the "Further North Express", applied to a Fridays only afternoon train from Inverness to Wick and Thurso, stopping only at principal stations, and which ran from 1906 to 1915. The name was also at times applied to the corresponding southbound train on Thursday mornings. From 1913 the "Further North Express" ran also on Wednesdays northbound and Saturdays southbound.

As a very general outline, the pattern of train service over the Perth-Inverness main-line over many years offered a night train with sleeping cars from the south, leaving Perth around midnight; the morning mail making only a few stops, followed by another about 9am omitting some stations; a mid-day all-stations train and another serving most stations in the late afternoon. There were also locals to Blair Atholl in early morning and evening, the latter with a through carriage to Aberfeldy. Southbound services corresponded.

Station buildings on the Highland varied considerably, from the small cottage-type building incorporating the stationmaster's dwelling commonly used in the north, (as seen in the illustration of the viaduct over the Kyle of Sutherland), to the pattern usual for the stations mainly south and east of Inverness, (as in the illustration of Pitlochry). This latter design was basically two blocks with gables facing the platform and the roadway behind, joined by a narrower section with a verandah over the platform between the end blocks one of which usually had a bay window. The gables were frequently corbie-stepped and incorporated "H.R." in the stonework of the one, with the date in the other. Some of the later stations of this pattern were of timber construction and had hipped gables (as in the illustration of Tomatin), while at smaller ones a simple timber building with a ridge roof, (as illustrated by Culrain), or even a flat roof sloping to the back, were provided for station business. There were many variations.

Places such as Aviemore, Forres, Dingwall, and of course Inverness, were more ambitious, while Strathpeffer was unusual with its long timber building and saw-toothed glass verandah over the platforms. (This station, including platform and trackbed, has been preserved and now serves as a craft centre).

Station footbridges were distinctive, with a graceful flattened curve over the line, and it may be noticed that the run of the straps on the sides of the stairs was unusual. (A drawing of the H.R. footbridge will be found in *LMS Architecture* by Anderson and Fox, O.P.C., 1981). The notice affixed to them read: "Passengers are to Cross the Railway by the Bridge only". The footbridges and other ironwork such as the water columns, were supplied by various firms, much of it from the Rose Street Foundry of Inverness, which was situated on the left bank of the river opposite the harbour quays; there was no railway connection to it.

The footbridge at Forsinard station, showing detail of construction. The notice is not the original. This view shows the line climbing towards the County March. Note the signal cabin on the platform controlling the north end of the loop.

*D.L.G.H.*

# OPERATING THE LINE

The Highland, from a very early date, had adopted the telegraph "block" system between stations so that only one train was allowed to run between adjacent stations at one time. The working timetable laid down the stations at which each train was to cross another running in the opposite direction, and any alteration due to late running, etc., could only be authorised by the Line Superintendent's office at Inverness. Indeed the whole of the traffic was controlled by telegraph Orders from and to that office, known from its telegraph call-code as "the P.T." The arrangement seems to have worked very effectively, although the wires must have been heavily engaged. The Board of Trade nevertheless thought single-line railways should use the staff or tablet system to ensure greater safety, repeatedly pressing the Highland to do so, but the company claimed it was unsuitable for long lines and continued their existing arrangements.

In 1864, however, the Board of trade did secure an undertaking from the Highland that "one engine only or two coupled together will be allowed in steam between " (two specified stations) "at one and the same time". Pressed on the matter yet again in 1890, Andrew Dougal, the General Manager, replied in the usual tone;

> With regard to Electric Tablet or Staff system, I have to remark that the Block System of working has been in use on this line since its commencement, 35 years ago, and has been found in every respect satisfactory. My directors are not therefore prepared to make any change seeing that the expense would be considerable and no benefit would be given to the public".

Up to this period the Highland was frequently at variance with the Board of Trade. Alterations to track layout at various stations were not reported to the Board of Trade for their approval, as they were required to be. The marshalling of mixed trains has already been mentioned, and under their powers in the Regulation of Railways Act 1889, the Board of Trade ordered the Highland to comply with their requirements in that respect (and others) by August 1893, but still the Highland stalled. The matter seems to have come to a head following an incident near Achterneed on September 25th 1897, when a broken wagon coupling on an ascending mixed train allowed the tail of the train including the passenger carriages to set off backwards down the hill, with only the guard's hand-brake available. A high speed was reached before the train came to a stand on the level near Dingwall. Fortunately, no one was hurt, but some level-crossing gates were smashed. Soon after this, on October 19th, the Highland instructed its staff to marshall mixed trains with the passenger carriages next to the engine, although it is questionable even then whether the instruction was always carried out.

The reason for the earlier recalcitrant attitude up to that time seems likely to have been at least partly due to the characters involved. Andrew Dougal had been General Manager and Secretary from early days and was a man of great character, if at times a little autocratic, and he expected his departmental officers to get on with their jobs unhindered by him. Murdo Paterson, the company's engineer since 1874, had in fact built most of the system, the earlier parts in conjunction with Joseph Mitchell, and was also a great leader and of an independent disposition. Both were highly respected in the community. With such confident Scottish characters in command it is perhaps not surprising that attempts by officials in London to tell them how to run their railway were unwelcome: after all they seemed to have been running it very well. However, Andrew Dougal chose to resign at the end of 1896, and his successor Charles Steel remained for only two years. David Jones, the Locomotive Superintendent, resigned on account of failing health, also at the end of 1896. Then Murdo Paterson died suddenly at Culloden on August 9th 1898. The company could ill afford the loss of these stalwarts, but relations with the Board of Trade became more normal thereafter. There is a saying that new brooms sweep clean!

The tablet exchanging apparatus. The table stood 5ft above the ground pedestal, the 1ft 11in. long operating arm being pivoted 9 ins below. Occupation of the single-line section required possession of the relative tablet: the apparatus illustrated enabled it to be picked up at speed. *A.G. Ellis collection*

In 1897 the Highland decided to adopt the tablet system in the form of Tyer's No. 6 tablet instruments, and issued instructions on working that system to the staff in that year. The earliest sections of line so equipped were Portessie and Buckie, Alves and Hopeman, Strome Ferry and Kyle of Lochalsh, Aberfeldy and Ballinluig, Aviemore and Daviot, and Keith and Mulben, all these being in operation by the following year. On the main lines, Manson's tablet exchanging apparatus was installed, the crossing loops being arranged to permit smooth running at high speeds, although previously one line had sometimes been straight with the loop diverging at both ends, when so far as possible, the straight line was to be used for both directions for trains not stopping there. Usually, particularly in the north, the tablet instruments were located in the booking office where levers were also provided to operate slots on each of the starting signals. This was to enable such locations to be worked by one man, called a pointsman by the Highland.

Most of the crossing loops were of considerable length, so making necessary the provision of a cabin at each end to work the points. Each cabin, in addition to working the points and signals at the relative end of the loop, also slotted the home signal at the opposite end of the loop and worked an inner distant arm below that home signal. This inner distant, called a repeater arm on the Highland, was also controlled by the same lever in the booking office that operated the starting signal for the direction concerned. Having accepted a train from the next station in rear, and if no train was approaching from the opposite direction, the pointsman could go to the cabin at the opposite end of the loop, set the points and pull off the starting signal and inner distant (repeater) signal levers and the slot lever on the home signal, although none of these arms would then drop by reason of their other slots. Proceeding next to the cabin at the end nearest the approaching train, he would then set the points and lower the home and outer distant signals. Then to the booking office when, having received acceptance from the station in advance, and withdrawn the tablet, he could pull the starting lever thus removing the slot and allowing the starting signal and inner distant (repeater) signal to clear.

When the train had arrived and duly gone forward, the pointsman might go first to the cabin at the entry end of the loop and put the outer distant and home signals back to danger before restoring the starting lever in the booking office and the levers in the cabin at the other end of the loop. In the interval between visiting the first cabin and restoring the starting lever in the booking office, the home signal would be "on" and the inner distant below it "off"; an unorthodox signal display! There was an instruction in the Appendix to the Working Timetables that this was not to be allowed to happen but nevertheless it was sometimes seen. Some men used their bicycle to speed their journeys between the cabins.

Until 1921 the outer distant applied only to the home signal, the inner distant or repeater arm being pulled off only for a train not stopping at the station and using the tablet exchanging apparatus. The driver of an approaching train unable to use the apparatus when normally expected to do so was to sound two "crows" on his whistle, while if an engine failed to pick up the tablet, the driver was to sound one long and two short whistles, and having stopped, the fireman had to go back for it. Station staff were expected to bring it towards him to save time.

Forsinard station office, showing the two "starting" levers, with tablet instrument for Altnabreac to the right and telegraph instruments in the left-hand corner. The second tablet instrument for Kinbrace has been replaced by the L.M.S. with a train staff instrument seen in the centre. *D.L.G.H.*

If the tablet was lost - and it sometimes happened - a pilotman had to be appointed to conduct the traffic through the single-line section until the lineman came to adjust the instruments and insert in them a ticket recording the number of the lost tablet and prohibiting its use or insertion into the instruments again by anyone but himself. There were some places where a different arrangement applied, the signal cabin being located towards the end of the crossing loop where any sidings were connected. The points at the other end of the loop were then operated from a small ground frame with release and back locking by a lever in the signal cabin.

To gain access to sidings it was necessary at many stations to draw off the loop on to the single-line ahead, and to allow of such movements without withdrawing a tablet and lowering the starting signal, a shunting arm in skeleton form carrying an "S" was provided. Lowering this arm authorised a driver to draw ahead

Typical Highland Railway signal cabin, at Scotscalder, with a platelayers' hut alongside. Note the absence of a nameboard, regarded as unnecessary at such places; note also the flat Caithness countryside.                          *D.L.G.H.*

Highland Railway bracket signal at Rose Street signal cabin, Inverness. This view taken in L.M.S. days clearly shows the H.R. form of construction, the architraves, and McKenzie & Holland finial.
*D.L.G.H.*

sufficiently for this purpose only (Rule 46). Although this was not to be done if a train had been accepted to approach on the single-line, Rule 36 required a driver approaching a distant signal at danger to "bring his train to a stand thereat and then proceed cautiously towards the home signal, being prepared to stop if necessary", so providing additional safeguard. In July 1917 this was amended to "...bring his train quite or nearly to a stand and thereafter proceed cautiously..."

In earlier days a number of collisions, mostly minor although sometimes involving injuries, occurred in such circumstances, where for some reason an approaching train ran past the distant signal to collide with an engine shunting on the single-line. For example on March 28th 1894 the 05.20 up mixed train from Helmsdale, with the wagons next to the engine, proceeded past the distant signal at Tain at danger and collided at about 10 mph with the engine and twelve wagons of a down goods train which was outside the up home signal preparatory to shunting back to the sidings. There were no injuries of consequence, but the Board of Trade inspector claimed that the practice was a breach of the company's undertaking of 1864 that "one engine only or two coupled together will be allowed in steam between Edderton and Tain at one and the same time", but the company claimed that their stations extended from the down distant signal to the up distant signal. The Board of Trade was still complaining of this practice and also of unbraked wagons in front of carriages of mixed trains, into the present century.

Another circumstance which gave rise to a number of collisions was that the lever in the signal cabin at say, the south end of a crossing loop, which slotted the home signal at the north end, could not be pulled unless the points at the south end were set for a train approaching from the north. In these circumstances a train from the south over-running its home signal would be pathed into the wrong side of the loop if a train had been accepted into the loop from the north.

In the 1890s the necessity to so set the points was being removed, and at Newtonmore the alteration to the interlocking of the levers had been made on August 1st 1894. However, the following day, the staff not yet having been told of this, the pointsman set the points at the south cabin for the up side of the loop as he had hitherto to do, before allowing an up goods train into the loop at the north cabin. At the same time, because the down distant signal wire was unduly tight, that signal was falsely off and the approaching down express, running late, over-ran the home signal and into the up side of the loop to collide with the goods train. The circumstances were ironic for, from that very day, it was no longer necessary to so set the loop points if only the pointsman had been so advised. The result was one of the more serious accidents in the annals of the company, causing a passenger to be killed for the first time on the Highland, and six others injured.

Highland Railway bracket signal with shunt arm at Forres. Arms for shunting movements were of skeleton form and carried an S.      *D.L.G.H.*

Bottom of a typical Highland Railway signal post, showing "slot" levers, lowered lamp, and windlass. The windlass barrel is 3½in. diameter, ratchet wheel 8in. diameter, and handle 10ins long. *D.L.G.H.*

Top of a typical Highland Railway signal post, showing lamp-hoisting chain and pulley. The lamp has been lowered to the bottom for trimming. Note the unusual finial.                                                                                        *D.L.G.H.*

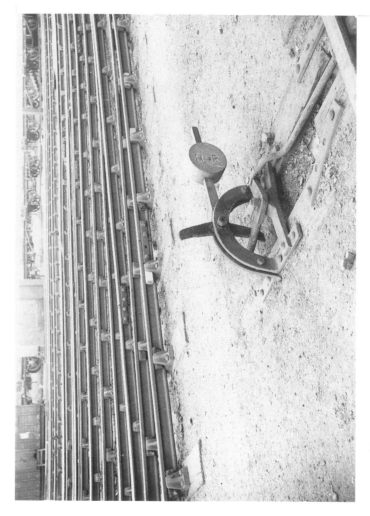

Highland Railway hand point lever. This example is at Inverness near the site of Welsh's Bridge.

*D.L.G.H.*

A ground disc signal at Blair A-holl. These were mainly used in sidings.

K. Fenwick

The long stretches of single-line raised problems. The heavy holiday traffic each summer rather swamped the Highland's necessarily sparse facilities, while in winter there was snow to contend with. Many striking photographs have been taken of engines charging snowdrifts, especially in Sutherland and Caithness, although Dava, between Forres and Aviemore, was regarded as the worst spot. On one occasion at Dava, passengers survived a few days blockage by eating a consignment of fish, the guard having received permission for this after managing to tap on to the telegraph wire to Inverness.

Snow blowers between Kinbrace and Forsinard. To the uninitiated a cursory glance could be deceptive as related in the text! *D.L.G.H.*

Clearing a snow drift in Caithness.

*D.L.G.H. collection*

Snow ploughs were kept at all the locomotive sheds, and the van of a "Snow Plough Special" always carried a good supply of whisky, as well as foodstuffs, for shovelling squads. Snow fences and "blowers" were erected at many locations. The blowers were timber erections in the form of slanting screens alongside the line. There is a story of a doctor new to the district, driving between Kinbrace and Forsinard - where, for part of the way, the railway and road are fairly close together - and noticing the snow blowers, anxiously reported to the Forsinard stationmaster that there was a lot of fencing blown down on the line! A similar blower to obviate drifting sand near the coast was erected on the Burghead branch.

In the north of Scotland in those days, the Sabbath was held in great respect and the Highland was not expected to provide a train service on Sundays. Nevertheless, the Post Office insisted on a mail train each way between Perth and Inverness, Forres and Keith, and Inverness and Wick, with connection to and from Thurso. These trains were also available to passengers but when, in 1920, the Post Office no longer required them, they disappeared from the timetable. There were no goods trains on Sundays, the Working timetable quoting "Goods trains will be run on all lawful days". The inclusion of one from the south arriving at Inverness early on Sunday mornings and, for a time, another departing from Inverness for the south at 11pm on Sundays could apparently be overlooked.

Between 1897 and 1911, several additional crossing loops were introduced to help speed up operations. In some cases, crossing loops were switched out at night so that one of the home signals at these had a second arm on a bracket to direct trains through the "wrong" side of the loop, and a different shaped tablet used between the stations on each side in these circumstances. Between Slochd and Daviot both the intermediate crossing loops at Tomatin and Moy could be switched out together.

Four of these additional crossing loops were used only during the summer months when traffic was so much heavier than during the winter. At the end of the summer season their cabins were closed, the points and crossings taken out and then restored again the following year. These were Dalraddy (between Aviemore and Kincraig), Inchmagranachan (between Dunkeld and Dalguise), Moulinearn (between Ballinluig and Pitlochry), and Etteridge (between Dalwhinnie and Newtonmore). There was also a permanent crossing loop on this section at Inchlea, nearer to Dalwhinnie. The bleak and isolated cabin here had its stair enclosed within the building.

At the end of the First World War the peak years of summer traffic had passed and these extra crossing loops and their cabins were removed entirely. (The LMS restored them for the heavy traffic during the Second World War, with a single brick-built cabin near the mid-point of the loop). Over the years, sidings to serve quarries, distilleries, etc., were added at several locations on the single line, access being gained by insertion of the tablet for the section in a ground frame. A siding with a different purpose was Loan, half-way up the hill between Achnashellach and Achnasheen. It was provided in case an up train could not manage to the summit and had to be divided. Subsequently, on February 1st 1918, a crossing loop was also provided here but closed again in 1920 and removed, as was the refuge siding some time afterwards. The refuge siding could only be used when the crossing loop cabin was closed and the long-section tablet in operation.

The Highland Railway Rule Books did not follow the Railway Clearing House pattern of 1876 until the 'nineties. The 1888 issue still contained local Rules pertaining to the Clachnaharry swing-bridge and the Inverness Harbour branch. Trains ran in accordance with the Working timetables issued to all outdoor staff in early summer and October, and sometimes more often. Planned out-of-course operations and alterations were notified by the issue of Special Train Timebills and Circulars as required, although it was frequently necessary to resort to a telegraph message to all stations concerned in any "last minute" alteration. The telegraph was the normal means of communication in those days although telephone communication between adjacent stations became available over the tablet instrument wire, a switch being turned at both stations to achieve this when a call signal was given on the plunger.

On September 1st 1897 the first Appendix to the Working timetable was issued and this effectively consolidated much necessary information, although the Working timetables included a great deal of operating information also, e.g. the stations at which the various trains were to shunt as necessary to attach or to put off wagons for specified types of traffic, and in earlier years, the detailed duties of pilot engines. The Working timetables of the 1870s even included the rates for all kinds of traffic, and details of conditions applying to various kinds of tickets and passes, and also cloakroom charges. There were further issues of the Appendix in 1901, 1907, 1916, and 1920. Following the issue of the 1897 Appendix, the Special Train Timebills were superseded by a Weekly Programme of Special Trains, as from May 24th 1898, but these sometimes required one or more Supplements and even telegraph messages were often still necessary.

This small wagon turntable with extended rails was located just outside *Dunrobin's* shed at Golspie.                    *D.L.G.H.*

Such Supplements or telegraph messages might be required for an outing at short notice by the Duke of Sutherland with his private locomotive *Dunrobin* with or without his saloon from his private station at Dunrobin Castle, north of Golspie. Although a private station, and open only during the summer season, the fares book quoted fares to most Highland stations and to some others in Scotland and England also. When closed, trains might stop to put off parcels for the Castle. The third Duke had largely financed much of the line north of Inverness and indeed had built the Golspie to Helmsdale length entirely. He liked to drive his engine himself on occasion but nevertheless employed his own driver, Alex. Rhind, who had been a driver on the Highland before, when aged about 25, taking up employment with the third Duke in 1870.

The Duke's engine had originally been kept at Brora, but when the fourth Duke obtained a new and larger *Dunrobin* engine in 1895, he built a new shed for it and a house for its driver at Golspie, where Alex. Rhind became a well-known personality, remaining the Duke's driver until 1917. The saloon had its shed at Dunrobin station. Most of the Duke's trips were to Inverness, e.g. for meetings of the Board of Directors, but other points on the northern section were visited too, including Kyle of Lochalsh. *Dunrobin's* journeys in 1904 will give an idea of the use made of it, although there may have been additional trips made at short notice:

| | |
|---|---|
| January 7th. | To Inverness with saloon and H.R. brake van for luggage, and return light engine. |
| May 21st. | Light to Inverness and return with saloon (which had been to the south). |
| May 25th. | To Inverness with saloon, return later. |
| August 17th. | Light to Inverness, returning with H.R. composite and brake. |
| August 22nd. | To and from Wick with saloon. |
| Sept. 7th. | To Inverness with saloon, then to Invergordon. |
| Sept. 8th. | Returning to Dunrobin from Invergordon with saloon. |
| Sept. 28th. | To Inverness with saloon, then light to Dornoch. The saloon was attached to a director's special to Dornoch, from where *Dunrobin* brought it home. |
| October 7th. | To Inverness with saloon and H.R. brake third, returning with saloon empty. |
| October 17th. | To Inverness with an East Coast Joint Stock saloon and brake van, returning light. |
| Nov. 21st. | To Inverness with empty saloon, returning with passengers and H.R. brake van for luggage. |
| Dec. 19th. | To Inverness with saloon, returning light engine. |

The Duke of Sutherland's engine *Dunrobin*. Its shed can be seen behind.
*A.G. Ellis collection*

On September 1st 1906 a rather different trip for *Dunrobin* involved running light to Helmsdale to collect some dogs for the Castle, these being accommodated in a H.R. brake-third attached for the return journey. An earlier, even more unusual arrangement, was the hiring of the Duke's original little engine by the H.R. on Saturdays, or later Fridays, in the summers of 1878-85, to run an ordinary passenger train from Golspie to either Wick or Thurso and back.

Many other matters required the issue of notices to staff, and these appeared almost every other day, dealing with such varied subjects as rates, revised or special fares, lost or missing luggage or parcels, lost season tickets, calling in specified old wagons for scrapping, alterations to signals, returns on tickets, cash collection, station house rent, etc. In most cases the notice ended with a curt "Acknowledge receipt". A few examples may be of interest although only extracts from these can be given here:

| | |
|---|---|
| 25/1/98: | Code of engine whistles to be used at Elgin. |
| 18/2/98: | Certain signals disconnected at Aberfeldy; hand signals will be used meantime. |
| | Complaints re - breakages of eggs. |
| | Camels conveyed in horse boxes to be charged at horse rate. |
| 21/3/98: | Vehicles labelled "Not to go" must not be moved until Loco. Dept. proclaim safe. |
| 6/4/98: | Electric train tablet to be introduced on Hopeman branch from April 11th. |
| 7/4/98: | Alteration of points and signals at Inverness station, Welsh's Junction. |
| 18/4/98: | Muzzling of dogs. |
| 19/4/98: | Seating of local passengers to be in Highland carriages, not through carriages. |
| 21/4/98: | Reservation of compartments for use by fishsellers. |
| 28/4/98: | All fish trucks to be withdrawn from goods circuit and confined to passenger traffic from May 2nd. |
| 5/5/98: | A new signal to come into use on May 9th at Black Tank 2¾ miles north of Struan to protect rock cutting excavation work for the doubling of the line. |
| 9/5/98: | The age limit at which puppies are to charged as such to be six months. |
| 28/6/98: | Instructions and forms to be used for a wagon census to be taken at 12 noon on Sunday July 10th. |

Finally, in full, a more homely one of January 2nd 1899 :

"The General Manager informs me that representations have been made to him from several different quarters that it would be a great convenience and advantage to the Public were they able to obtain a Cup of Tea or coffee at any of our Stations, and he has asked me to take the matter in hand. I shall be much obliged if you will kindly give it your careful consideration, so far as your station is concerned, and let me know whether any one in your neighbourhood would be willing to undertake such".

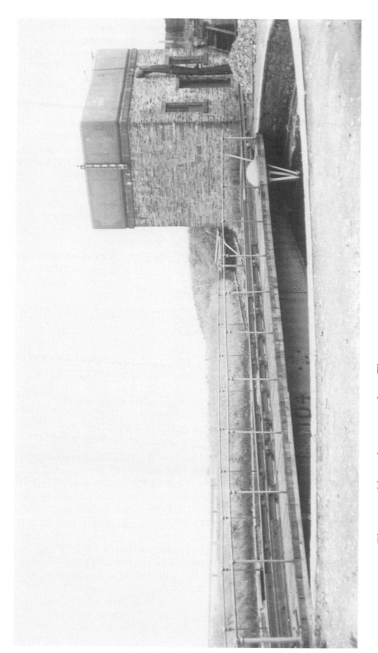

*D.L.G.H.*

The turntable and water tank at Thurso.

The mass of detailed instructions in the Appendix to the Working Timetables included signalling procedures, carriage lighting, heating and cleaning, local speed limits or running times between certain stations, including a rather indeterminate one: "The speed of Goods trains on any portion of the Skye line must not exceed 25 to 30 miles per hour". Other instructions included codes of engine whistles to be used at junctions and yards, stations where tow-ropes were allowed to be used for shunting; stations and yards where engines could take water, and should no water be available, a notice to be displayed at the next watering station each way "No water at ...", with a green lamp at night; dealing with passengers in a state of intoxication; stationmasters instructing staff, especially new youths, who were "to be polite and respectful to passengers". On night trains the guard was to collect tickets at the stations where the night man would be engaged on other duties - no doubt referring to signalling; on local holidays guards were to keep first class carriages locked to prevent third class passengers taking possession of first class carriages while there was ample accommodation in third class coaches; the engine working at Invergordon Harbour was to be limited to 3 mph and preceded by a man with a red flag.

The names of district permanent way, signal, telegraph, and locomotive foremen, were given and also the diameters of the turntables at various places. In 1920 these were:

| | |
|---|---|
| Perth 54ft 9ins. | Dingwall 43ft 6ins. |
| Blair Atholl 55ft 3ins. | Fortrose 50ft. |
| Kingussie 50ft. | Tain 50ft. |
| Aviemore 55ft. | Lairg 50ft. |
| Grantown 48ft. | Golspie 21ft. |
| Keith 50ft 4ins. | Helmsdale 55ft. |
| Portessie 45ft. | Georgemass 46ft 3ins. |
| Forres 48ft 6ins. | Wick 55ft. |
| Inverness 63ft 4ins. | Thurso 51ft 11ins. |
| Muir of Ord 50ft 1 in. | Lybster 46ft 3ins. |

Kyle of Lochalsh 50ft.

Also given were the maximum loads to be taken by the different types of engine over the various parts of the line. These were too complicated to quote in detail here, but it may be noted that a "Clan" class engine could take 240 tons over Slochd and Drumochter; and twice that load between Aviemore and Kingussie. No goods train was to exceed fifty wagons, and such a load could be taken by the various six-coupled main-line engines including the 0-6-4Ts, on several sections of line. "Clan" class engines were not allowed north of Inverness, and neither they nor "Castles" or "Jones Goods" 4-6-0s had any load rating east of Forres. Only "Glens", "Bens", and "Skye Bogies" were suitable for the Skye line. "One engine in steam" applied to the Fochabers, Fort George, Fortrose, Dornoch, and Lybster branches.

Breakdown vans with, among other equipment, "Stroudley's ramps", were available at Perth, Blair Atholl, Aviemore, Forres, Inverness, Dingwall, Kyle of Lochalsh, Tain, Helmsdale, and Wick. The company's 15-ton steam crane was, of course, stationed at Inverness. Built by Cowans, Sheldon in 1887, there is some evidence that it was intended for an Indian railway, but not delivered, so the Highland may have acquired it at a bargain price. It could lift 15 tons at 25ft 6in radius when jacked down, or 10 tons free. It was carried on four axles and, with a warping drum on each side, was a versatile and useful machine.

The Highland Railway breakdown train; built by Cowans, Sheldon in 1887.
*D.L.G.H. collection*

During the winter months, stationmasters sent weather reports to Inverness at 8am and 5pm. There were many instructions on methods of working at specific places. In one of the earlier issues there is an intriguing reference to guards being guilty of mutilating their flags "especially the green one". Was there a religious significance?

Some other features of Highland Railway practice should be mentioned. Although the Highland loading-gauge was fairly tight, a feature missing from the smaller goods yards was a fixed loading gauge. Local stations were provided with a 15 foot pole for checking the height of loaded wagons by radius from each rail in turn.

The engine of a train which was to be followed by a special, or that of a relief train running ahead of the regular train, carried over its left-hand buffer an oval red board lettered "Engine Following". Engines did not carry headcode lamps, only a lamp at the chimney, but a lamp was also carried on each side of the tender - or cab of tank engines - both of which displayed a white light in the direction of travel and a red light in the opposite direction. Shunting engines within station yards and sidings carried only the lamps on the cab sides but in this case the lamp on the right hand side of the engine showed a red light towards the front of the engine and a white light towards the rear. The lamp on the left hand side showed a white light to the front and a red light to the rear.

Some of the signal cabin bell codes were different from those used by other companies, e.g. acknowledgment of "Train entering Section" and "Train Out of Section" was one beat.

The Highland Railway was careful to have all its sundry material branded; not only hand lamps, guards' whistles, refreshment room crockery, etc., bore the company's name or initials, but even such minor items as pen nibs and pencils. Strangely however, the company's Trespass warning notice did not give any indication of its ownership; the heading was simply "Notice" and the wording finished merely with "By Order of the Directors". Most Trespass warning notices were off-white enamelled plates with chocolate coloured lettering, although some were cast iron. The same colours were used for other such plates and for station name-boards which were carried on two posts surmounted by small finials. Boards on which Highland Railway posters were displayed were headed "The Highland Railway via Dunkeld", and often had a rounded top. Staff uniforms followed the orthodox styles, although stationmasters, excepting those at the main stations, latterly wore a "pill box" type of hat with "silver" braiding including the initials "H.R." Porters' caps had a scarlet band on which "H.R." appeared in black block letters. Despite all this, much crockery apparently went astray, and carriages were to be searched when luncheon baskets, which had been provided at Kingussie, were retrieved at Aviemore and Dalwhinnie.

Ticket platforms were provided outside the main terminal stations, and unless tickets had been collected at the previous stopping station, all passenger trains stopped thereat for tickets to be collected. This was because the Highland did not have any corridor trains, although there were a few H.R. corridor carriages on through trains to the south in the company's last few years. Carriage doors were to be locked at the previous stopping station so that passengers could not escape at the ticket platform! In the case of trains from the north approaching Inverness,

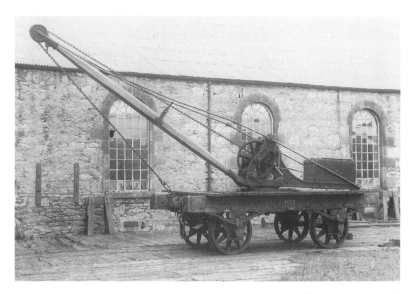

Travelling hand-crane at Inverness carriage and wagon works, not equipped to go beyond the works. Note the dumb buffers. *D.L.G.H.*

A hand-operated goods yard crane at Halkirk. The lifting capacity is not shown. *D.L.G.H.*

Clachnaharry station was used as the ticket collection point. In earlier days, some intrepid ticket collectors saved time there by climbing along the footboards from compartment to compartment as the train travelled, inevitably fairly slowly, between there and Inverness. For trains from the south and east there was a ticket platform at Millburn junction.

Highland Railway tickets were quite colourful, the main types in the 1900s being:

| | |
|---|---|
| 1st Class Single; | White. |
| 1st Class Single, Child; | Top half yellow, lower half white. |
| 1st Class Return; | Outward half yellow, inward half white. |
| 1st Class Return, Weekend; | Outward half white with vertical red bar, Inward half pink, with vertical white bar. |
| | |
| 3rd Class Single; | Green. |
| 3rd Class Single, Child; | Left ⅔ pale green, remainder white. |
| 3rd Class Return; | Outward half buff, inward half green. |
| 3rd Class Return Weekend; | Outward half pink, inward half blue. |
| 3rd Class Return Day Excursion; | Top half of both outward and inward halves white and lower half green. |

The outward half of return tickets originally was the left hand half, but in the 1890s this was reversed and in the case of the weekend and one-day excursion tickets the outward half was then overprinted "O". Two other examples were: Dog tickets pink, and Bicycle tickets buff, overprinted "B". Before second class fares were withdrawn in 1893, these tickets had been, single - blue; return - outward half heliotrope with vertical red band, inward half cream with vertical blue line. Paper tickets of larger size were used for various purposes, such as military personnel, circular tours, excess fares (red), staff and other passes, etc.

As passenger services were necessarily infrequent, travel in the brake van of goods trains was permitted provided the passenger signed an indemnity form and paid the first class fare. The up night goods, 1 am from Wick, seems quite often to have carried one or two passengers between various stations, and this facility on this train remained available until 1939.

At some places the railway bridge was the only local means of communication across a river. The high viaduct over the River Oykell at Invershin on the line to the north was one such place, and for many years a halfpenny fare was available between the stations at each end of it, viz. Culrain and Invershin, half a mile apart. Doubtless there were illicit crossings on foot on occasion.

An interesting aspect of travel on the Highland in earlier days was that the reservation of seats was discouraged. "Stationmasters must, without giving offence, discourage as much as possible applications for Reserved Seats, which has a continual tendency to delay trains by the way". Nevertheless, stationmasters could send an application for a reserved seat or reserved compartment for the appropriate number of passengers, to the Traffic Manager who, alone, could authorise such reservations. However, such restrictions disappeared after the First World War.

Carriages with coupé end compartments were fairly common on Highland trains. These usually had ample windows in the ends, but, because of the proximity of the next vehicle, these did little to assist the passengers enjoy the scenery. If it was immediately behind the engine there would be some little advantage but these carriages were not to be so positioned in a train, and if one had to be, the coupé compartment was to be locked up to prevent passengers using it, probably in case of coal falling from the tender breaking the end windows.

With so many through carriage workings from the south, Highland trains could present a motley appearance, but, in an attempt at uniformity on the branches, the allocation of the carriages used thereon was painted on the solebars. To facilitate operations at Perth and further south, carriages leaving Inverness were to be marshalled in the following order: Glasgow (Queen Street), East Coast route, Waverley route, other North British Railway stations, Caledonian Railway stations, Midland route via Carstairs, Manchester, Liverpool, Euston, other West Coast route stations south of Warrington, East Coast route via Larbert, Waverley route via Larbert, North British Railway stations via Dunblane. Many of these would represent only occasional workings. A similar scheme applied to fish trucks but specified the English destinations in more detail. On trains from north of Inverness any through vehicles for the Forres direction preceded those for the Carrbridge line.

The telegraph instruments always remained an essential part of the company's communication system, and all station staff had to master it. The telegraph messages were condensed by the use of code words of which there was an extensive list common to most railway companies, although the Caledonian did not use it. The following are a few examples:

| | |
|---|---|
| Undermentioned train will not run, advise all concerned; | CAPE |
| Instruct driver and guard of following train to stop at station named, to take up or set down undernoted party; | CELT |
| A special train will run as under, advise all concerned and note; | CICERO |
| Have pilot engine in readiness to attach to following train; | COLORADO |
| Be prepared to detach undermentioned, leaving here in rear of following train; | COW |
| Single timber truck; | MACAW |
| Undermentioned cannot take duty, Arrange; | MINT |
| Send supply of loco. coal (by) first means; | SNIPE |
| Goods brake van; | TOAD |

(Some of the rolling-stock terms persist today).

On the other hand, less urgent railway business was dealt with by written "bills" which were copied in or pasted in a letter book. These included a weekly return of any occasions on which tow-roping was used and the reason therefor; replying to the Traffic Manager's enquiries regarding delay to a train, passenger's complaints, ticket and parcel irregularities, staff arrangements, accounts, and many more mundane items.

The arrangements for the conveyance of Post Office mail bags and parcel baskets were detailed in the Working Timetables, and were quite complicated. In some cases there was a station-to-station bag, and also a few interesting routings, such as a late bag from Dunkeld to Perth which was sent on a down passenger train to Ballinluig, where it was transferred to an up goods train for Perth which did not stop at Dunkeld. A Highland Sorting Carriage was included in certain trains between Perth and Inverness, also Inverness to Bonar Bridge or Helmsdale.

Over most of the route of the Highland Railway the Post Office telegraph wires were carried on the same posts as the railway's wires, although the Post Office wires took their own direct route north of Helmsdale to Wick and Thurso. Over the railway route between Helmsdale and Wick there were two H.R. telegraph wires, and the Post Office at Wick used these for Post Office business to the H.R. stations on that section, the stationmasters acting as sub-postmasters.

# A FAR FLUNG OUTPOST

Brief mention should be made of the Invergarry & Fort Augustus Railway which ran to the latter place from Spean Bridge on the North British Railway's West Highland line to Fort William. Despite being so far removed from the Highland Railway's system, the Invergarry & Fort Augustus Railway Company's line was worked by the Highland Railway from its opening on July 22nd 1903 until 1907, when the Highland relinquished its ten year lease in favour of the North British, who eventually bought the Invergarry & Fort Augustus Railway.

This was a single-line with crossing stations at Gairlochy, and Invergarry, and controlled by electric train staff instead of tablet. It was relatively lavishly laid out, and at the Fort Augustus end there was a ¾ mile long branch to a pier on Loch Ness which necessitated a swing-bridge over the Caledonian Canal at the top of the Fort Augustus flight of locks, and a large lattice girder bridge over the River Oich. The swing-bridge was left open at night and on Sundays, being interlocked with the Pier branch staff.

There were four daily journeys, one of them "mixed", and three of them continued to and from the Pier until services were withdrawn from here after September 1906, the Pier branch thereafter being disused. One engine was normally sufficient to work the Invergarry & Fort Augustus Railway but there were occasional additional special trains necessitating a second engine so the 4-4-0T normally based at Fort Augustus was at times supplemented by 4-4-0 No. 48. 4-4-0Ts Nos. 52 and 54 saw duty at Fort Augustus.

The normal branch train consisted of one third, one composite and a brake van, with a spare first being kept at Fort Augustus. Transfer of stock to and from the Highland at Perth involved quite a long journey. It is probable that after 1905 such movements to and from the branch went by the new Caledonian line via Crieff to Balquhidder, then Crianlarich, and on to the North British to Spean Bridge.

The Invergarry & Fort Augustus Railway. H.R. 4-4-0T Locomotive No. 54 at Fort Augustus Station.

*D.L.G.H. collection*

# A LOOK AT WHAT WENT ON

When Thomas Wilson came from the North Eastern Railway in 1898 to be General Manager of the Highland Railway, he issued a circular to the staff which illustrated the way of life on the Highland at that time; it is surely worth quoting in full:

Inverness, 27th June, 1898

I desire to enlist the assistance of the staff in improving the character of the Highland line for punctuality; the Railway from which I come is proverbial for punctuality so far as its local train service is concerned, so much so that it is a common saying with travellers - "If you go to a North Eastern station a minute after a train is due to leave, you will be certain to find it has gone". I am not unmindful of the difficulties of running the Highland trains punctually, difficulties which do not exist to the same extent on other Railways, but I am convinced we shall be able to make a sensible improvement.

The first point I wish to impress upon the staff is that punctuality is a rare thing on the Highland line. I do not know whether the staff have realised this. Usually our trains start late, lose time on the road, and arrive late at the end of the journey; this does not appear to be because the trains are too tightly timed. So far as I have observed, several of them are allowed too much time, and this will be attended to in due course, but in the meantime, we must make a serious endeavour to run **the trains at the advertised time.** Those of our staff who have travelled over other railways will have noticed a marked difference in the manner in which the trains are dealt with at the Stations. The public are quite familiar with it, and the moment a passenger from another Railway passes on to the Highland line, he seems to take for granted that there will be a "leisureliness" which would have excited surprise on other Railways; whilst local passengers are permitted to wander up and down the platforms instead of being requested to take their seats the instant the train stops. Great improvement may be made in this respect by a sharp and polite "Take your seats, please". When the public recognises that an earnest effort is being made to run the trains with punctuality, they will appreciate it.

I am afraid that on the Highland line we do not attach sufficient importance to the value of fragments of time. There are 29 stations between Perth and Inverness, and 39 between Inverness and Wick, but I fear it has not been realised that if a train from Perth to Wick loses only half a minute at every Station, the result on the whole journey is a loss of over half an hour; but when not half a minute is lost but several minutes, the total loss of time is most serious. I wish to remind staff that before a train draws up to a Station, everything that forethought can suggest should be prepared, and the instant the train stops, everyone should be anxious to get it started on its way without the loss of a second.

I do not propose to go into detail to show what can be done to secure punctuality - I prefer to leave the detail to the intelligence and experience of the staff; and besides, there are general regulations with which the staff are familiar. The only instruction I give in this Circular Letter is to the Station Masters, viz. that whenever a train has a late start, or whenever time is lost at a station - if a train arrives one minute late, and leaves two minutes late - a report, giving the explanation, must be made to the Office of the Superintendent of the Line, without waiting for an official enquiry.

I make no reference to the penalties for indifference, etc. I do not like penalties, and prefer to appeal to the Staff in their own interest, and for the credit of the Service, to assist in making the Highland Line one of the most punctual - having due regard to its drawbacks - in the country.

But a look at a stationmaster's responsibilities as reflected in the reports and letters written by one at a remote spot a lifetime ago may put the foregoing into perspective. To set the scene, the sixty miles of railway between Helmsdale and Wick ran through very sparsely populated country without as much as a village on its route, apart from Halkirk, about a mile from Georgemass Junction. The crossing stations averaged 7½ miles apart and some of them can have provided little traffic. Altnabreac for instance was at the end of a rough track winding through the moors for twenty miles to Halkirk and serving only two shooting or fishing lodges in the vicinity.

On the other hand, Forsinard station, although it had nearby only a shooting lodge, a hotel, a little school and a handful of scattered cottages occupied by estate or railway workers, was situated where the railway, having so far accompanied the route of what is now the A897 road to the north coast, turned eastward and crossed the road to head for the County March and Caithness. So Forsinard could be quite a busy station, for the road - in those days very rough and narrow (although the Highland Railway's Tourist Guide called it "good") - passed several scattered crofts on its 16 miles onwards down Strath-Halladale to Melvich on the north coast, where there were other small fishing communities and fishing lodges. Powers had been obtained in 1898 for a Light Railway branch from Forsinard to Melvich and Port Skerra but the line was never built.

At times there would be a good measure of traffic in fish and in peat, and always a few passengers, augmented in the summer by the fishing and hunting estates' proprietors and their guests from the south, as well as other holidaymakers. In late summer there were always two or three livestock sales held at Forsinard which often each attracted some thousands of animals from the crofts and estates down the Strath and along the coast, and which would be railed south after sale.

So let us look at the resulting rail activities at Forsinard. Being a watering station, there was a large tank at the south end of the loop and a column at the north end. The level-crossing, the two single gates of which were manipulated in turn on foot, was situated on the loop between the water-tank and the platforms, the goods shed being south of the level-crossing on the down side. The station building incorporating the stationmaster's house was on the down platform.

From reports to the Traffic Manager, we learn that few first class tickets were issued from Forsinard to stations to the northwards, and that the two copies of the public timetables supplied for sale were usually returned unsold. Many reports referred to ticket irregularities or to payment of accounts, for such matters were very tightly controlled and every penny counted.

Cheap return tickets were available from Glasgow and Edinburgh on Tuesdays and Fridays to Wick, Thurso, and to Lybster, but these were not issued to the local H.R. stations. On one of a number of occasions, the stationmaster at Forsinard reported

> "Party holding the enclosed Cheap Return tickets 240, 241, Buchanan Street to Thurso alighting here refused to pay the Thurso fare as I have customarily collected, saying she never paid such before although coming off here every summer with same tickets. Please instruct me."

Followed three days later,

> "The difference between Glasgow fare to here and cheap fare to Thurso is 4/5½d. each ticket, whereas it has been the general rule to charge the fare between here and Thurso, viz. 2/4d. Please instruct as to this".

Then, on the matter of a child's fare,

> "I have seen Mr.---- and (he) asks how we know the boy's age, and declines to pay the extra amount until we are able to prove the correct age of his boy".

Somewhat similarly,

> "I saw no Dog with a passenger joining train here. It must have been taken into train under cover".

Inverness would on occasion call for all trains to be checked on the following day; one such inspection resulted in the following:

> "All trains checked and found correct but passenger on 8.40 am held ticket Wick to Glasgow without date (Had it dated); Edinburgh and Glasgow excursion tickets on 5.40 am and 9.50 am trains not clearly dated - merely a blot. On 8.40 am Guard --- without pass."

The water column at the north end of Forsinard station. It was supplied from a large tank near the south end of the station, which served the up trains. *D.L.G.H.*

Sometimes errors occurred here too of course, e.g.;

"Tickets not dated; I regret having missed to do so and discovered my mistake afterwards and endeavoured to get Helmsdale, but failed".

Two mail bag mistakes were reported thus;

"As is usually the case, mail bag was placed at door of van by guard and (the door) being opened, I took such out on to the platform, when it was then taken to office by Postman, who, too late, train being away, it was seen it was Kinbrace to Thurso bag we had; our bag was then discovered thrown out of train about starting signal".

"I beg to report a Parcel Post Bag labelled Glasgow to Invergordon having been received here off 9.40 am today. It was duly returned by 2.50 pm train and Invergordon advised".

When a station audit showed two tickets missing and the stationmaster debited with their cost although clearly they had not been used, he pleaded "it is hard to ask me to pay for what the Coy. has had no loss".

On occasion an intending passenger would request that the "express" would be stopped for him, and this would have to be referred to Inverness to arrange if agreed. Then there might be a request for a motor car van to be provided to load a visitor's car. Forsinard was once host to a North British Railway saloon conveying a special party, and during the week it was there, a clean towel for the return journey had to be obtained from Edinburgh.

Another long reply to the Traffic Manager referred to two "gentlemen" with bicycles who left them at Forsinard one Sunday while they went on to Altnabreac by train, returning the next afternoon without notice, which they had promised to give. The guard, abiding by the rules, refused to take their cycles as they were not labelled ready to put on the train with them. What the two "gents" from the south said is not recorded, but provoked the guard to remark "Some of you think we are all dogs here in the north". The stationmaster claimed "They got nothing from me but civility". The cycles were to go forward by the first train the next day, but a car-load of passengers arriving at the last minute, they were forgotten, and so went with the afternoon train, with 2/- to pay.

A simpler although rather surprising reply to another complaint was

"This was a box of Eggs and marked such 'With Care'. I civilly told Mr --- that he could not get such as luggage with him, not being personal luggage, so he agreed to send box by cheapest way, which was by goods train. Copy invoice attached".

The following was perhaps intended to stall enquiry;

"On arrival of 2.45 pm train yesterday, a man alighted here (a bit the worse of liquor) saying he was carried past Georgemass for Thurso. He could not find his ticket but said he had one Wick to Thurso. He went

Highland Railway trespass notice, at North Road level-crossing of the Skye line at Dingwall. This is one of the enamelled pattern with chocolate coloured letters on an off-white background. The cast-iron version carried the same words and was otherwise similar to the weight restriction notice shown in the next illustration.

*D.L.G.H.*

to Hotel for tea and was to go back by 1 pm Goods train, but I believe he altered his mind owing to lateness of train and stayed overnight in Hotel. I did not see him today until 9.40 am was about due, when he returned with his Wick ticket. He is Mr ---, Commercial Traveller, Thurso, and I believe is well known there".

Complaints of another kind related to damaged goods, e.g. a bag of sugar refused by the consignee for being very wet, apparently conveyed in a leaking van. Again, a consignee in the south refused to accept, and pay for, boxes of fish. The stationmaster pleaded on behalf of the senders

> "These fishermen are very poor and live from hand to mouth and I have no doubt it is the want of means that prevent them remitting, which they consider very hard, having lost all their fish and paying cartage for --- miles.

The Post Office too would sometimes complain of delay to their telegrams, e.g.

> "You will observe that Wick doesn't say when this message was offered me. I was in office at 9.40, got block for 8.40 at 9.44 and departure at 9.48, when I went to close gates and set signals for train, returning to office at 9.58, when Altnabreac told me Wick had a message for me, and said he only began to call at 9.55".

Many reports were concerned with delays to trains, sometimes of only a few minutes. The reasons were usually straightforward but sometimes elaboration ensued, such as an occasion when the stationmaster felt the driver did not really need to "waste time" taking water when there was a full supply at Helmsdale, and gave rise to an argument between guard and driver. But in another report, the situation was rather different -

> "30 minutes delay to 2 am Fish special; I questioned pointsman as to the delay and he informs me Guard could not be got out of his van. The fact of the matter is he was drunk and sleeping accompanied by one of the Wick porters. The shunting on of the wagon of fish was performed by pointsman and enginemen".

Of course, there were sometimes other kinds of explanation.

> "Through the breaking of North Home signal wire while pulling off for 10.25 am up Express today, that train was detained about 4 minutes outside before being flagged in".

A tablet failure was reported thus

> "Herewith please find Pilotman's ticket received ex-Altnabreac by 12.30 am today, which had to be issued through failure of Tablet Instrument at 1 am today; and at 8.20 am upon again testing instrument it came alright; Cause of failure no doubt was atmospheric currents".

Cast-iron weight restriction notice at Thurso. The locomotive shed of typical
H.R. style can be seen on the right with the turntable and water tank in front of
it, and the station in the left background.                              *D.L.G.H.*

A more human cause appears in another such incident;

"Delay to 8.40 am. I am sorry for this happening; I was unexpectedly called away to Goods Shed on loading bank and mistook the time I had before coming back for taking on train ... Pilotman's ticket herewith".

Another report regarding tablets;

"I have to report that the 1 am train of today arrived here with only part of the tablet Altnabreac and Forsinard. On pointsman enquiring re- the matter he was informed by trainmen the tablet got damaged and engine ran over it. The piece has been sent to Lineman who adjusted the instrument in time to admit of 8.40 am train coming on."

Illustrative of how important were the pennies was a long argument between the stationmasters at Forsinard and Scotscalder about the charge for a pail of milk, one claiming 4d. while the other wanted 6d., alleging that a letter had been enclosed within the address label. A ticket to Bournemouth was entered at 32/2d. (£1.67), and as it should have been 32/3d., even that penny (½p) was followed up.

The pointsman's hours appear to have been 3.30pm to 3.30am, but late running trains could mean overtime for which the stationmaster would have to seek payment for him. The pointsman was once sent sixteen miles on his bicycle to endeavour to collect a small overdue account.

There being no shop of any kind near Forsinard, the railwaymen's wives went periodically to Wick or Thurso for provisions, Inverness sending a pass for their necessary journeys. The stationmaster had to ask Inverness to send silver in proportion to each surfaceman's pay as he could not obtain change at Forsinard for the total amount sent.

Living at Forsinard could be hard in winter and from time to time there would be requests for repairs or improvements to the station house. The following report on the loco water tank is interesting:

"Please have the heating of water tank here looked into; it is only lately I was aware that there is about 3 inches of concrete in bottom of tank over plates which makes the open fire below of little use in keeping off frost; two years ago we have had as much as 28 to 30 inches of ice in tank".

Another problem was getting the children of the surfacemen living in the cottages at the County March to school at Forsinard. The four of them walked the three miles down the lineside and, there being two underline bridges with no side protection, it was felt that they could be endangered. Two suggestions were made; the 8.40am train to stop and pick them up, or "the section man could run them down by bogie before the 8.40am train passed Scotscalder without the prescribed six men ..." We do not know how it was resolved.

A livestock sale gave rise to a very busy day, (and of course for the hotel too!). There would be a prior request for the services of a clerk and three men for loading, surfacemen usually fulfilling the latter, as well as for about 30 trucks and vans: an engine would be sent for shunting and it would sometimes work away a special train in the evening. The stationmaster would be busy persuading buyers to rail to the south "via Dunkeld".

After one sale the stationmaster reported

"It was well after midnight ere I could go to rest for the night. On passing to house I found two people fast asleep on seat outside station, one of whom (had) purchased Goods train ticket from pointsman ere arrival of 1pm Goods. The other (had) asked for drover's ticket but pointsman informed him he could not do so. I do not know when his stock was loaded but I think he ought to have seen to his ticket ere 1am following morning..."

Another little bit of excitement, not on a sale day, is reported:

"Bull arrived here off 5.40am with invoice for Congested Districts Board. He seemed quite quiet and all right but with no ring in nose and a very short rope (only about seven feet). After being untrucked and delivered to man in charge, who seemed a bit timorous, he got off from him and gates being closed, he turned off onto Dock bank and before anyone could get in front of him he sprang onto rails, breaking one of his hind legs. Men in charge wired --- of C.D. Board for instructions who in turn wired to have Bull put in Hotel Stable where he now is; also said he had wired --- Veterinary Inspector, Wick, to come by first train".

Much more could be quoted from these Reports but the foregoing must suffice. Although there may have been one or two misfits, the Highland really was quite a "family" concern, at least on the ground. That there was dissension in high places on occasion is evident, and the clash of engineering personalities in 1915 is well known, when F.G. Smith's new "River" locomotives were prohibited by Alexander Newlands, the Civil Engineer.

In earlier days an annual "soiree" was held at Inverness, but as the system grew and numbers expanded, had to be cancelled about 1890. (In this connection it is interesting to note that, when the centenary of the opening of the Inverness & Nairn Railway came round in 1955 and BR were unwilling to recognise it, Inverness Town Council wished to, and in conjuction with a public exhibition and slide-show, organised such a reunion, much of the credit being due to Miss McDougal, the town's librarian. Endeavour was made to contact and invite all surviving former Highland Railway staff, and a good time was enjoyed by all; the oldest participant was 94. It was a commendable effort in which the writer was privileged to participate).

When the Highland entered its last week of its separate existence at the end of 1922, the Weekly Programme of Special Trains included a Special Notice to the Staff which is worth recording.

"On Monday next, 1st January, the Highland Railway will become part of the London, Midland and Scottish Railway.

The passing of the old Highland Railway Company is such an important event that it calls for a few words from me of personal thanks to the Traffic Staff generally. I am deeply grateful for the loyalty, good-will, co-operation and assistance which the Staff have always given to me as Traffic Manager during the last 21 years.

The organisation under the new grouping of the London, Midland and Scottish Railway has not yet been arranged, but you will be officially advised as soon as the Management of the Highland Section has been definitely settled. In the meantime I am asked to carry on as at present, and you will therefore, until further notice, report to me as usual.

I appeal to all members of the Traffic Staff to demonstrate, by every means in their power, that in taking over the Highland Railway, the new Group have got possession of a live concern, serving a wide district which under progressive management, is capable of great development.

The Staff can best serve the new Company by taking a keen and intelligent interest in all that makes for the material welfare of the Company, by the exercise of that courtesy to the public which is characteristic of Highlanders.

A disposition to be obliging to passengers and traders, combined with the smart handling of trains, will do much to attain the best results. The wonderful work overtaken by the Highland Railway during the Great War can be maintained, and even improved upon, during peace time if all concerned make up their minds to live up to the creditable record which they have already achieved.

With cordial greetings and best wishes for the new year.

Thomas McEwen,
Traffic Manager's Office,                    Traffic Manager".
Inverness, 29th December 1922.

# THE 1914-1918 WAR.

About a quarter of the Highland's staff joined the Forces in the 1914-1918 war, and 87 lost their lives. The war had a tremendous impact on the Highland, probably greater than on any other railway company, giving rise to intense traffic that stretched resources to the limit and beyond, so that several locomotives and many wagons had to be borrowed from other railways.

There were substantial developments around Invergordon which became a major Naval base. From 1915 a "pug" (i.e. small tank engine) was sent daily from Dingwall to shunt there, taking with it a carriage for staff from Alness. In January 1918 Great Western Railway steam railcar No. 45 with 64 seats arrived for this untimetabled duty: on days when it was not available for use the Highland again had to provide a locomotive. The railcar was offered for sale to the Highland at the end of 1919 but the offer was declined.

Subsequently, siding accommodation was greatly increased at Invergordon: Dalmore distillery became a Naval workshop a new branch being laid to it for the Admiralty from a new junction about half-way between Alness and Invergordon, worked by a ground frame secured by the tablet lock, and called Belleport. Another new Admiralty line led back from the Admiralty sidings at Belleport, along the shore to the Invergordon harbour branch. These lines were worked by the Admiralty's own locomotives, three Stroudley 0-6-0Ts bought from the London, Brighton & South Coast Railway in January 1918, formerly L.B.& S.C.R. Nos. 638, 681, and 683.

A new branch was laid in record time, across fields to Inverness harbour for ammunition storage, and a United States Naval base was established off the Muirtown branch, which was taken over by the U.S. Navy. Rails from the Keith-Portessie branch were used for these works, which were all abandoned after the war and removed by 1924. The Admiralty had another two engines on these sidings, ex-L.B.& S.C.R. 0-6-0Ts Nos. 637 and 679. (During the Second World War, green Stroudley tank engines again appeared on former Highland Railway metals; Southern Railway 0-4-2Ts Nos. 2358 and 2699 worked variously at Inverness, Dingwall, and Wick).

The Skye line was also taken over by the Admiralty, the Highland being allowed to run only one daily train each way for passengers and mails. The Admiralty worked their trains over it with some 4-4-2T locomotives borrowed from the London & South Western Railway. The Strathpeffer and Kyle of Lochalsh hotels were also occupied by naval personnel. On the main-line there was the vastly increased goods traffic and the Euston-Thurso Naval special, which commenced on February 15th 1915 and ran every weekday until April 30th 1919, normally of fourteen carriages and somtimes duplicated.

Military guards were posted at tunnels and important bridges and viaducts, some 25 locations in all. Drivers had to sound their whistles to warn them of their approach. From July 25th 1916, members of the public had to obtain a permit to travel beyond Inverness, and access to trains was controlled accordingly. Trains from the south and east had to have all carriage doors locked at their last stop so that passengers could be detrained under control at Inverness.

But all that passed, and on January 1st 1923 the Highland Railway was absorbed into the London Midland & Scottish group, and although some of its unusual operating features continued to apply for another twenty years or more, it was now a different organisation beyond the limits of this essay. It is nevertheless pleasing that the memory of the Highland Railway is being well preserved by the present day interest in it.

## POSTSCRIPT

For anyone not familiar with the north of Scotland a railway journey to Wick, Thurso, and to Kyle of Lochalsh offers something new and worthwhile. The scenery remains enchanting as even the bleak moorland around the various summits of the line has its appeal. Although all the branch lines, the old main-line over Dava, and many of the smaller stations have long since gone, there is still plenty to interest the railway enthusiast. The trains themselves and the motive power are of course very different, and radio electric token working north and west of Dingwall has removed all the old signalling, so the scene there is quite changed. Go and see it while you can.

No. 54 *Clan Stewart* gliding into Broomhill Station with an Inverness to Aviemore via Forres train in 1921. *J.L. Stevenson collection*

# FURTHER READING

| J.E.C. | *The Iron Track through the Highlands.* 1921. |
| Pratt. | *British Railways and the Great War.* 1921. |
| Ellis. | *Highland engines and their work.* 1930. |
| Vallance. | *History of the Highland Railway.* 1938,  rev. edn. 1972, 1985. |
| Allchin. | *A History of Highland Locomotives.* 1947 |
|  | rev. edn. by Tatlow 1979. |
| S.L.S. | *The Highland Railway 1855-1955.* 1955. |
| Nock. | *The Highland Railway.* 1965. |
| Hunter. | *Carriages and Wagons of the Highland Railway.* 1971. |
| Lambert. | *Highland Railway Album.* (2 vols). 1974, 1978. |

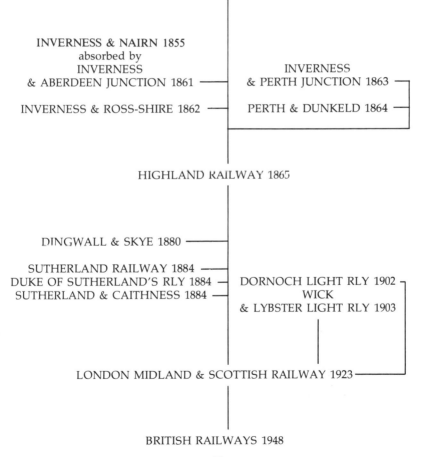

INVERNESS & NAIRN 1855
absorbed by
INVERNESS
& ABERDEEN JUNCTION 1861 ——

INVERNESS
& PERTH JUNCTION 1863 ⌐

INVERNESS & ROSS-SHIRE 1862 ——

PERTH & DUNKELD 1864 ⌐

HIGHLAND RAILWAY 1865

DINGWALL & SKYE 1880 ——

SUTHERLAND RAILWAY 1884 ——
DUKE OF SUTHERLAND'S RLY 1884 ⌐
SUTHERLAND & CAITHNESS 1884 ——

DORNOCH LIGHT RLY 1902 ⌐
WICK
& LYBSTER LIGHT RLY 1903

LONDON MIDLAND & SCOTTISH RAILWAY 1923 ——

BRITISH RAILWAYS 1948

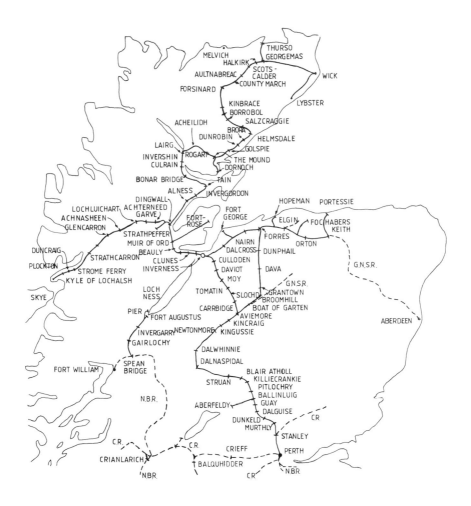

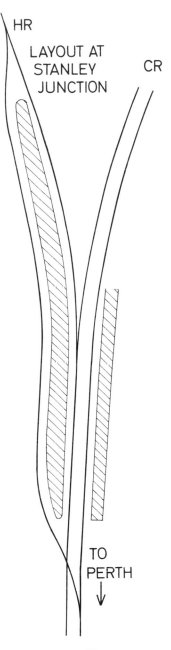

HR

LAYOUT AT
STANLEY
JUNCTION

CR

TO
PERTH
↓

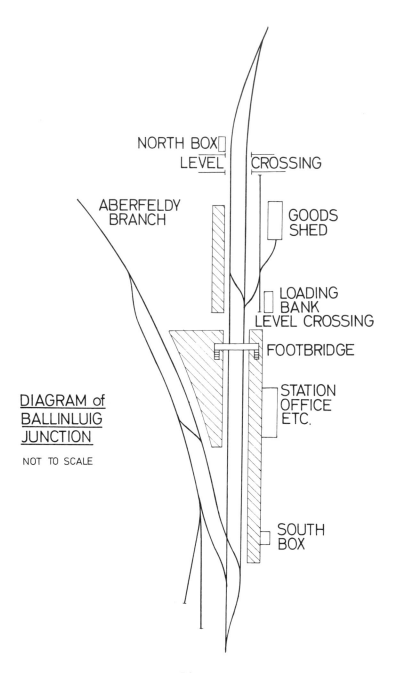

NORTH BOX
LEVEL CROSSING

ABERFELDY
BRANCH

GOODS
SHED

LOADING
BANK
LEVEL CROSSING

FOOTBRIDGE

STATION
OFFICE
ETC.

DIAGRAM of
BALLINLUIG
JUNCTION

NOT TO SCALE

SOUTH
BOX

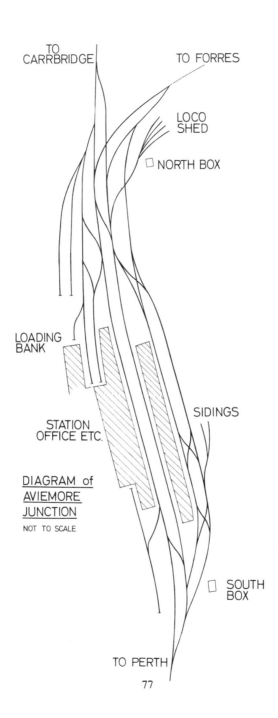

TO
CARRBRIDGE

TO FORRES

LOCO
SHED

□ NORTH BOX

LOADING
BANK

STATION
OFFICE ETC.

SIDINGS

DIAGRAM of
AVIEMORE
JUNCTION
NOT TO SCALE

□ SOUTH
BOX

TO PERTH

77

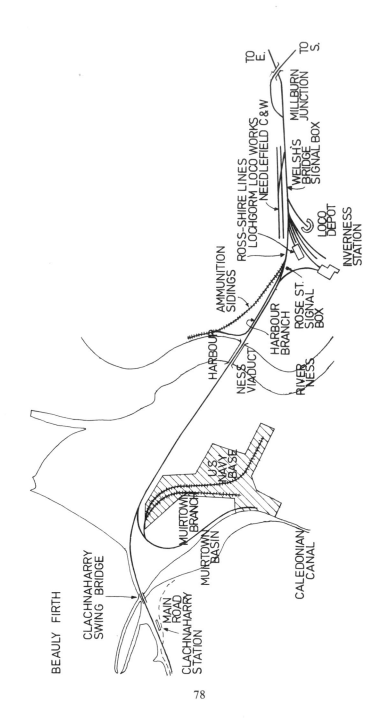

BEAULY FIRTH

CLACHNAHARRY SWING BRIDGE

MAIN ROAD

CLACHNAHARRY STATION

MURTOWN BRANCH

MURTOWN BASIN

U.S. NAVY BASE

CALEDONIAN CANAL

HARBOUR

AMMUNITION SIDINGS

NESS VIADUCT

HARBOUR BRANCH

RIVER NESS

ROSE ST. SIGNAL BOX

ROSS-SHIRE LINES

LOCHGORM LOCO WORKS
NEEDLEFIELD C & W

WELSH'S BRIDGE SIGNAL BOX

MILLBURN JUNCTION

TO E.

TO S.

LOCO DEPOT

INVERNESS STATION

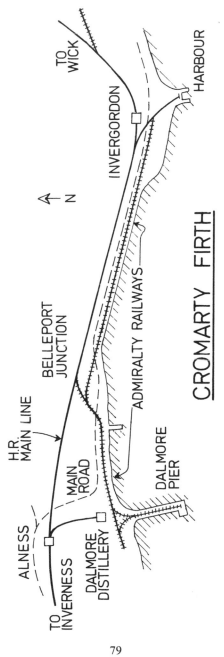

TO WICK

INVERGORDON

HARBOUR

N

BELLEPORT
JUNCTION

H.R.
MAIN LINE

ADMIRALTY RAILWAYS

MAIN
ROAD

DALMORE
PIER

ALNESS

DALMORE
DISTILLERY

TO
INVERNESS

CROMARTY FIRTH

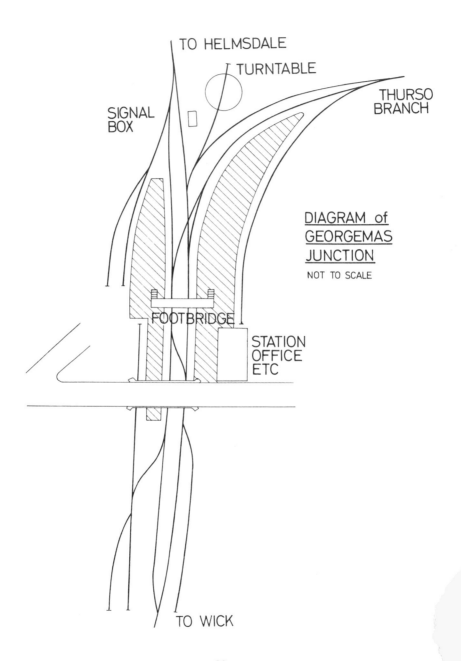

TO HELMSDALE

TURNTABLE

SIGNAL BOX

THURSO BRANCH

DIAGRAM of
GEORGEMAS
JUNCTION
NOT TO SCALE

FOOTBRIDGE

STATION
OFFICE
ETC

TO WICK